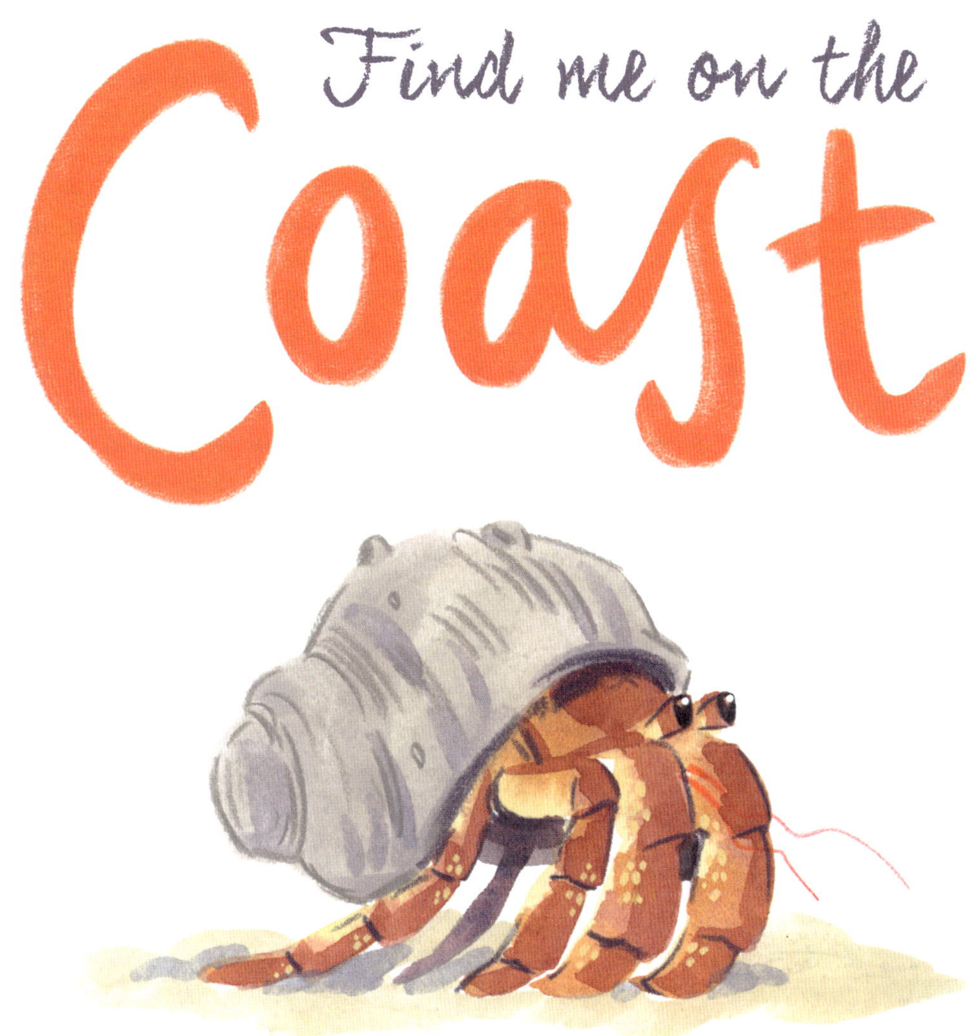

JESS McGEACHIN

Let's walk down a winding path to where the sand meets the sea.

This is the coast, and it wraps around all of the land on Earth.

It can be rocky, muddy, sandy and salty, and it's home to lots of clever creatures and fascinating plants.

On the beach, you might spy some shells.

Most shells are part of an animal called a mollusc. Over time, the shells will turn into sand and the wind will shape the sand into dunes.

Not this shell, though – a hermit crab is borrowing it to make a home.

Follow the footprints and you could meet a shorebird. These wonderful waders have adapted to coastal life in many different ways.

These stilts have tall legs to wade through marshy waters …

… and this curlew has a very long bill for poking around in the soft mud.

This oystercatcher is particularly proud of her bright orange bill. She's looking for lunch, and uses it to pry unsuspecting limpets off their rocks.

Night falls and a green sea turtle slowly makes her way up the beach. She's here to lay a clutch of eggs in the sand.

In a few weeks' time, her tiny hatchlings will look like this:

They'll have a dangerous journey back to the sea, but if they make it, one day they'll return to this very same spot to lay their own eggs.

On the coast, everything changes with the tide.

When the tide is high, the sea swallows up sand, rocks and everything else in its path.

When the tide is low, cracks and crevices fill with water and create rock pools.

These are windows into different worlds, each home to a new community swept in by the waves.

Rock pools are an excellent place for young animals to grow up. Their warmer waters are sheltered from the swirling ocean and full of delicious algae for fish to nibble.

But there's danger lurking here, too.

This octopus can change the colours and patterns on its skin to blend in with its surroundings.

Watch out, little fish!

Animals on the coast protect themselves in different ways.

This limpet keeps its soft body safe with one hard shell, a bit like wearing a bicycle helmet.

These chitons have eight shells that move together like armour.

Sea urchins wear a jacket of spiky spines to keep their enemies away.

Here are some sea squirts.

They protect themselves by squirting water if something gets too close.

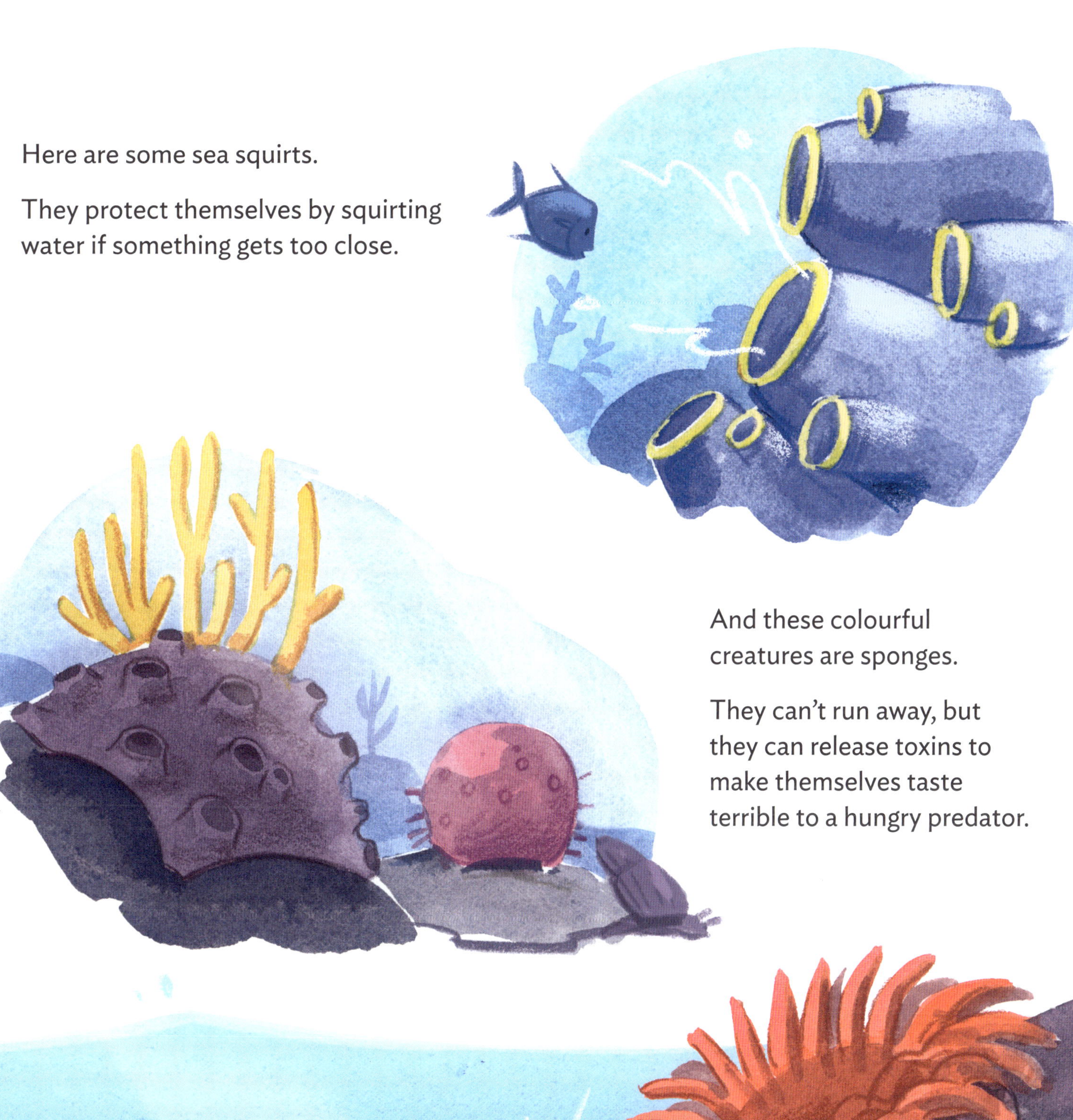

And these colourful creatures are sponges.

They can't run away, but they can release toxins to make themselves taste terrible to a hungry predator.

Whatever you do, don't tickle a sea anemone! They're very beautiful, but their tentacles can give a nasty sting.

It's heating up out here in the midday sun.

High on the tideline, barnacles trap water under their shells to create a cool indoor swimming pool.

Sea stars stick themselves to a rock with their hundreds of tube-like feet. They don't have to stay still, though – they can walk and even jump across the ground.

Many sea stars have five arms,

but others have eight …

or eleven …

… or even more!

On the sandy seabed, pairs of beady eyes watch and wait.

They belong to cleverly camouflaged bottom feeders like these rays and flatfish.

They stretch themselves out and glide along the sea floor. They have eyes on top of their heads to watch the world above.

Nobody does a better impression of a rocky carpet than this tasselled wobbegong shark, complete with its frilly, seaweed-like beard.

The view below the surface can look a lot like the one on land.

There are meadows of seagrass, where dugongs gently graze …

… and forests of
kelp, where weedy
seadragons hide.

Sea otters weave between the towering kelp.
They're searching for delicious sea urchins in the dim light.

Without the hungry otters, the urchins would eat everything in sight.
Nature knows how to keep things in balance.

Mangroves grow in warmer parts of the coast. These trees use their tall, arched roots to balance in the slippery mud.

Birds and lizards such as this mangrove monitor rest on the branches. The tangled roots make an excellent maze for young fish to hide.

If you like playing in the mud, you're in good company. Mudflats are home to colourful crabs of all shapes and sizes.

These little ones are soldier crabs ...

... and this is a fiddler crab.

This strange-looking fish is a mudskipper. It can breathe both underwater and on land, and it skips across the mud using its fins.

Proboscis monkeys swing through the swampy mangroves with ease.

The males show off with big, bright red noses.

They're also excellent swimmers …

… but now might not be the best time for a dip.

In cold parts of the coast, where rivers meet the sea, lie salt marshes.

These grassy wetlands fill and empty with the tide.

They're the perfect stopover spot for migrating birds like this great egret, who might get a snack to go if she's lucky.

This marsh periwinkle snail is climbing up a reed to make sure its one big toe doesn't get too wet.

Cliffs can be crowded homes on the coast.

These gannets spend most of their time at sea, but when it's time to find a partner and raise their young, only the best view will do.

Be careful not to steal someone else's spot!

Penguins mostly live on our world's southern coasts.

These little penguins are going fishing for dinner.

Puffins live in the northern parts of our world.

These puffins are digging burrows in the steep sea cliffs and lining them with soft grass. Here they'll raise their chicks, which are called pufflings.

Down on the rocks you'll spot slippery sea lions.

They spend time hunting at sea before waddling their way onto the rocky shore to rest.

Seals are more graceful underwater, where they swim with ease.

In the rock you might find fossils – impressions of strange sea creatures that lived on the coast long ago.

It looks like a storm's coming.

As our climate heats up, damaging weather is becoming more frequent, and we're losing parts of our coasts under the rising seas.

The animals who live here know all about change, but it's humans who are tipping things far out of balance.

The storm has passed and the tide has left a trail of treasure in its wake.

Look for clues about the animals who live on the coast, and make sure to leave the shells for the hermit crabs.

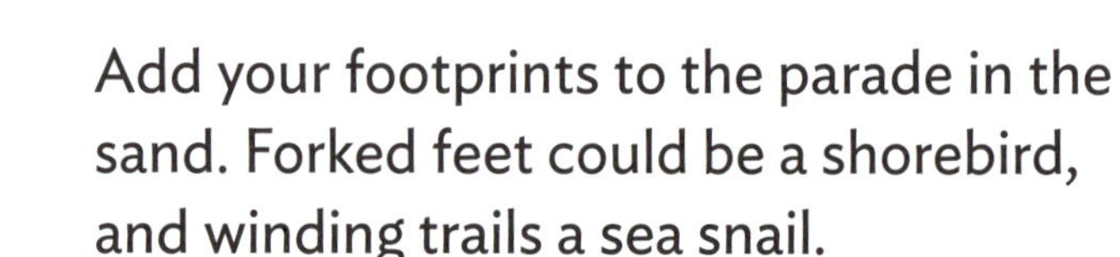

Add your footprints to the parade in the sand. Forked feet could be a shorebird, and winding trails a sea snail.

Sadly, you might spot rubbish, too.

There is a lot of cleaning up to do on the coast, so take rubbish with you if it’s safe.

The sun has come out and the water is warm.

What will you find on the coast?

Our world's coasts

We've just walked around the world's coasts. From sandy dunes to muddy mangroves, the thin sliver between land and sea is home to some of the most interesting life on Earth.

The creatures who live here can survive in extremes, but it's humans who are pushing things to their limit. It's our turn to change the tide and keep our coasts safe.

Salt marshes

Salt marshes are grassy wetlands that fill and empty with the tide.

They're a favourite place for fish to raise their young because they're protected from the rough ocean. Insects also love the still waters of the salt marsh, and other animals like eating the insects.

Coral reefs

Coral reefs are made up of large colonies of coral. Coral is an animal, not a plant, and it's very sensitive to changes in water temperature.

As our oceans warm up, our reefs are losing their colour and life.

Rocky shores

Plants and animals live in different spots on the rocky shore, depending on how often they like to get wet.

Some stay underwater nearly all of the time, while others only get the occasional spray of sea salt. The area between these two extremes is called the intertidal zone.

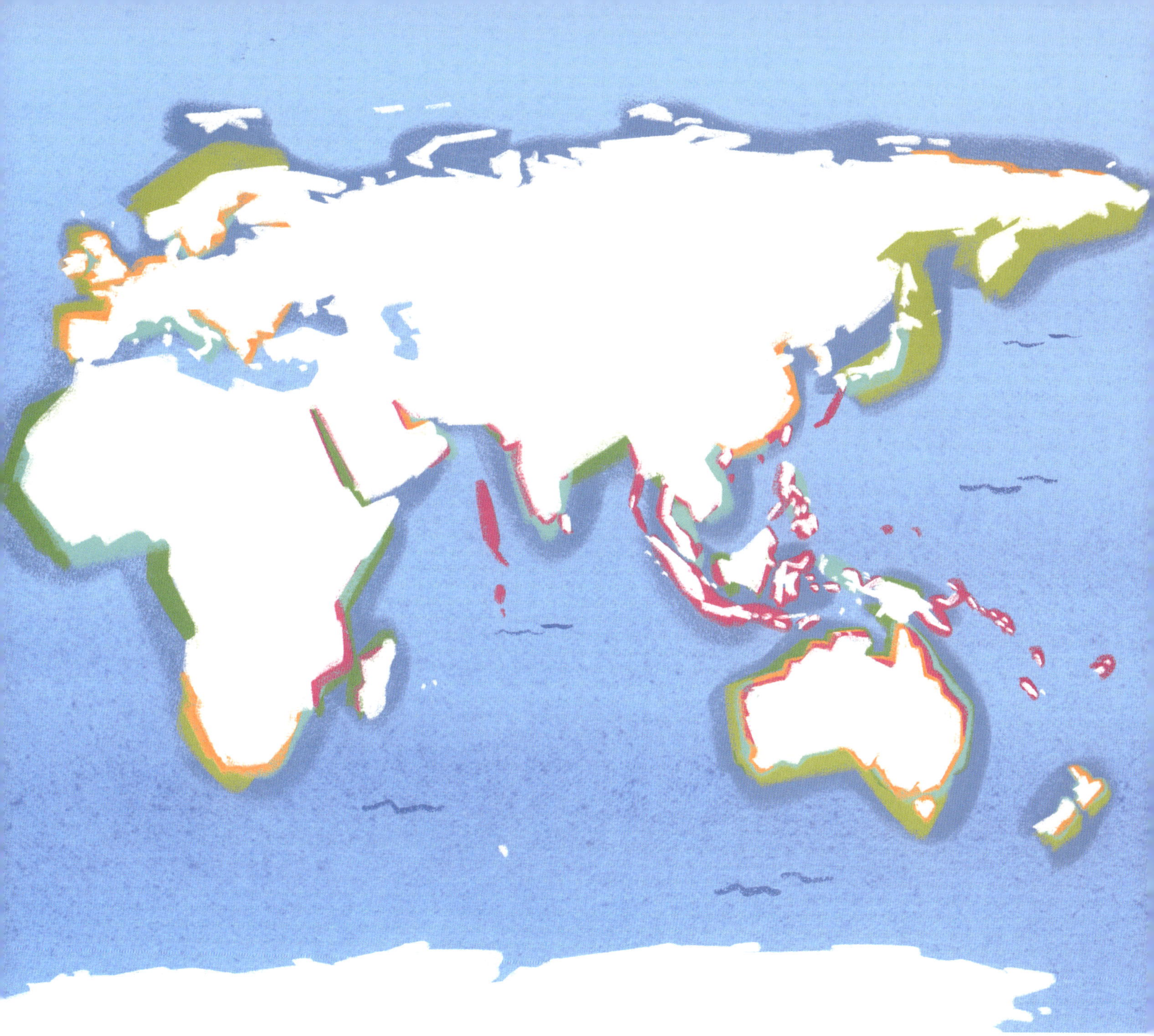

Mangrove forests

Mangrove trees grow in warm, salty water, where many other plants can't survive.

These forests are home to a range of animals, and their tangled roots protect the coast from erosion. They also store carbon in the mud below, which would otherwise contribute to climate change.

Kelp forests

Kelp forests are made up of tall, dense seaweed – a bit like trees on land. They grow in colder parts of the coast and provide protection and food to many marine species.

As our oceans warm, kelp forests are under threat from invasive animals such as sea urchins.

Seagrass meadows

Seagrass is an underwater flower that grows in lush meadows. These grassy beds are home to animals including sharks, turtles and dugongs. They act as a nursery for young fish.

Like mangroves and kelp forests, seagrass meadows store carbon and are incredibly important for the health of our ocean.

For my friend Angela, who loves the coast

With special thanks to Melanie Mackenzie, Caroline Foster, Alice Sutherland-Hawes, Jacquie Brown, Claudia Fletcher and Jeanmarie Morosin.

A Lothian Children's Book

Published in Australia and New Zealand in 2025
by Hachette Australia
Gadigal Country, Level 17, 207 Kent Street, Sydney, NSW 2000
www.hachettechildrens.com.au

Hachette Australia acknowledges and pays our respects to the past, present and future Traditional Owners and Custodians of Country throughout Australia and recognises the continuation of cultural, spiritual and educational practices of Aboriginal and Torres Strait Islander peoples. Our head office is located on the lands of the Gadigal people of the Eora Nation.

A catalogue record for this book is available from the National Library of Australia

ISBN: 978 0 7344 2363 4 (hardback)

Designed by Jess McGeachin
Colour reproduction by Splitting Image
Printed in China by Toppan Leefung Printing Limited